Flawed Cadaver

ab intra vol I

Dakota Jay

Dakota Jay

DEDICATION

This collection of poems is dedicated to you. To your smile. To your search for happiness.

- ARS GRATIA ARTIS -

Dakota Jay

CONTENTS

Dakota Jay

ACKNOWLEDGMENTS

I would like to sincerely thank my friends and family for their love, compassion, and support while I grow as a writer. Many thanks to Noel and Shane for the laughs and gaming nights. If I wrote down every one of your names, it would stretch longer than the book. So instead, please know from the bottom of my heart that you all add a piece to my soul. A special thanks to Mum and Dad, my three fantastic brothers, Gram and Popop, Yahweh, and every bright smile that passes my way.

An additional thanks to the lovely people who helped with the cover of my book: Matt Decker, Nick Keck, and Brenna Missimer.

PREFACE:
PRISM

This book has been quite the journey for me. It was daunting to sit down and start a book, especially since this will be my first.

I wanted it to be an art piece - for each and every poem to have a meaningful place in this book, holding dear memories, pains, and promises. So I decided to make it a journey to help me (and others) flourish. Everyone makes mistakes. Everyone has ghosts. So this is me trying to move past mine. Each chapter is represented by a colour, an idea, and me struggling to push onward. I wanted it to be organic, so it showcases my personal realization that I am far from perfect. The chapters hold the unedited thoughts of my life, with each poem being written by me through-out the last few years, up until the day I finally publish this book. Read on with an open heart, and enjoy it at your leisure. Peace and love.

BLACK:
SOMBER TONES

I am nothing if not a man of sin.
And I am hungering. For change. For anything.
...anything but this damned cage that I was born into.

Soft Covers of the Sun

Pulled along
The twisted chain of events
That some would call a life
(My life in actuality)
I find moments of sanity
Dripping from some source unknown

Further and further it goes
Possibly towards an enhanced existence
Leading me forward

Yet I stay,
Parching my lips with little wisdom

Intact I am understanding
But here I am nothing but the sins I eat

Two Thoughts

Helpless sits my heart

As I tear through the pathetic barriers
That I set years ago

I crave to feel alive
But living is rather scary
I crave to exit this scenery
But effort is rather scary.

Effort means that if I make a mistake…
I have no one to blame but myself.

And my heart cries to be heard.
It wants peace.

We both want the same thing.

I want to be at that end place NOW,
Living my dreams,
Writing without questioning 'why'
And breathing without worrying.

…but my heart knows better.
It takes time to go from this broken pit
Up to the tallest mountains
Where I can sit and see the world.

Oh God,
I want to understand it all.

Internal Interview

Nothing new
In terms of words to speak
With smiles
Or laughs.

I honestly wish to be left alone

To become myself,
Alone,
A hermit,
Avoided,
A heart,
Misguided

Me
That is me.

I am gagging
Coughing
Begging for air
And it is not enough
Without you here.

Oh poor me
Running through clichés
Living life betrayed
Is that not the world?

Well then you know my answer,
For I want nothing to do with this world.

Not You, But the Focal Point Beyond

Please
Anything
More
Please
More what?
I do not know.

More health?
Happiness?
Safety.

I hate my damning cage
Closing in daily
No time to breathe.

Money scares me.
Greed kills me.

Passion has no place
When I cannot last here.

Should I stop dreaming here?
I need to stop something.
Maybe I need the other side
The natural happiness that follows
...that follows after this place.

The Nature of Created Loss

The moving
The music can guide me forward
Through old twisted trails
That hush those with secrets

But I fear to open these maddened eyes

The branches tear at me

The forest mourns for me

The lost are all around
I hear them amongst the trees.
...

OH GOD

...

Am I equally lost?

Where and When

Heart heart
Clench my chest
Bleed while beating
Out comes red

I will still love you
I will still remember

When you grew too old
Realized I am bitter.

I lost my mind
It laughed away
It laughed some line
That I will never say

Rhymed thoughts lick my skull
A cavity
An empty hole

Bled me dry
Oh
Bled dry by me
I am lacking.

Oh God…
I am so lacking.

One day,
I truly hope you come back.
Without you
My soul burns
As it craves a notion
To bring forth light

…

I miss being a light.

Fingers Held Skyward

Judgmental skies
And I am no better.

The walls they echo
Earthly invitations
For splendor
For psychosis

The fathers
They cry
"Why am I still here?"
In bloody unison
As they drag chains
Of their selfish ways
To all ends of this earth.

And I am no better.

As the Rain Sways

A leaked invitation,
Outside my doorstep
Piled under the rain
And sadness of days past.

...this house has no better to offer,
No cheers to give,
To comfort the sky
With reasons to live.

So why not pick it up?
...
That is what I did.

And I wiped away the tears
From the sky's previous night,
Opening up the letter inside:

Written was a heart,
Searching for a sound of its own.
Written were some feelings,
Intricately woven somber tones.

The sky darkened and let out a damp sigh
And I suppose that I too then cried...

Because I had forgotten
Why this looked so familiar.

Maybe tomorrow I would have realized
That this letter was mine.
A second look, a second try.

But the wind has its ways
And like a dream it went drifting,
Drifting,
Drifting away.

Please forget your sorrows.
I guess we all have rainy days.

GREEN:
HOPELESS, BLOODLESS

My wretched eyes look down
See red
Everywhere but in my veins
See mistakes
Leaking out of my head
Oh God
How am I to change?

Video and Subtitles

Doctor,
Where is my heart?

Where are my lungs?

How am a breathing
When all I see before me
Are empty images
Of what I used to be?

You say I killed them all
The organs that lived in me
But all I remember is
The pain they used to bring

Maybe I am dreaming
Maybe I am dead

At this point does it matter?

I am a killer
Of self,
Of others.

Should I even ask for a second chance?
Would I even properly use a second chance...
Or would I go and burn myself again?

Doctor, dream me away.

It Felt As If Better, Momentarily

Time moved
In both directions
While I awaited
Ebb and Flow
Someone grab my hand
I do not mind the tide
Someone grab my heart
Wishing to feel
I wish to hear a new sound
Refreshing if it would be
A beating heart

And maybe like a match to another
I can be lit up too
Breathing in fresh lies
Breathing out old atrocities
(Maybe even a distant dream)

I am hollowed out
Scraped clean of idiotic hope
Scraped fresh of any home

I can breathe
But the tint of death
Rolls over worn eyes

Please comfort...
Please comfort my shaking hands

Washed Out

I feel as if
I should care more
Drink in the pain of the world
And get some joy in the long run
Understanding both ends of emotions

But currently I feel no emotional highs
Or lows.

Just... existing,
I suppose.

Creatures keep calling out
To endure this apathy
For some awful reason,
Surely.

And I try to keep this skin
From falling off

Things I Should Not Know

The air here.
Something new
Breathed in
Heaved out
Oh God
Clarity is a poison
Oh God
Am I really so awful?

So hollow?

Hollow, Hollow

Fingernails covered in dead
Searching through fresh thoughts
Still residing as flesh
Still glued to my eyes
The negative is proof
Still searching my eyes
For any reason to move on
To live on

I cannot understand

Why take back my heart
So used
So misused

I am a created monster
Full of hate for my own mistakes
I am a combination
Of all you could not achieve
Of all you could not say

Apparently I am worth nothing

NOTHING

I Am Lowered Into the Earth

I was drunk within your eyes
Lying inside the cornea,
Waiting for the world to leave me
So I could crawl out-
So I could plan my revenge
And preach my hypocritical lies.

No Knife Left

What happens when this is all gone?
All of it.

The money.
The lies.
The clothes.

Who am I when I am naked,
Curled up into a pathetic ball?

I am far from a saviour

I am the broken

I Am Lowered Into the Earth Pt. II

But now my tombstone reads:
"Here he lies
Here he will always lie
Like a pathetic man,
He corrupted love for lies.
So here he lies".

I am a wanted man,
I am the scum of the earth.

So why does this Savior love me?

...I am scum of the earth.

Romantic Cubicle

Bookshelves emptying
Day by day
Old thoughts scraping the surface
Once again
Only to be taken away,
Forgetting any light I once held.
Or why I held it.
Or why I chose you.

I asked "why"
Tears streaming out
And the shelves replied
In unison they cried
"You are decaying, son."

And I never went outside
Again.
Too scared to move
As my eyes strained
Forcing myself to notice
As more and more memories
Withered and left my side

I never pulled in another
Another thought
Another dream
Another idea to move with
Another hope to dance with.

I withered
Am withering.
Will wither.

Ongoing

RED:
CAPRICIOUS PARASITE

Who gave you the right to call me forever lost?
Capricious Parasite,
I will do everything to rid you from my mind.

Forgive me, parting sanity,
For I sometimes indulge in it.

Kill it Before it Thinks

The shaking begins
When I realize
That I might be fake
Mechanical,
Complex wiring

And they all smile
Astounded
As I say I live for redemption

Look at them applaud
"How wonderful"

But a machine cannot be redeemed.

So tear out this oil heart
Strip me of my fake actions
And give me desires
That showcase something...
Real.

I am the deceiver for now.

But one day I will lead
With a firm heart.

Tickets, Please

The crowd chanted
At me
To take action

Why else would they gather?

I sat on my windowsill
Knife in hand
I simply wished to rid myself
Of these voices that etch my skull

But they screamed at me to jump
Wanting a show.
They always want a show.

And although a knife
Would never solve my problems
And although jumping would shut them up
And send them home

I will not be their entertainment,
No,
Not anymore.

I will go back inside,
Break my mirror,
Focus less on perfection
And use what I have to become better.

I am not your entertainment,
No,
Not anymore.

Next Line Over

Dark lights
Dimming eyes
And instead of a spark
(Security to re-establish)
...
I am left with my own thoughts
Scratching the corners
The eyes
The twitching is natural
But this smile is not

Can I fall for something new
Can I trip into a whole new paradigm
Because beneath these painted masks
Holds more than just bitter lies

I swear.

But who am I swearing to?
And why does every inner struggle
Mar my shell
Burnt to a damning mess.

I suppose that I am just a mess
Who should not be left alone
Especially to his thoughts

Iron, Hide

Cut me open,
Drip me down,

Pull out a heart
That beats so loud.

Scream my thoughts
While red lines me

And I will dine
On broken dreams.

Guilty As Any Other

Why so headstrong?
Why so guilty?

Your mother raised you better than that.
Different than that.

Hung on a noose of starving morals
Anything to satisfy the hunger,
To curb the psychosis.

It was not always this way.
I tell my heart that.

...

But it was.
It was always this conflicting.

My soul cries out to be saved
From this venomous body

But I laugh.

I LAUGH
As sadness overwhelms what is left
Of this heart

Please God,
Save me

I Am Their Pivotal Sappy Story

Walk the line of thick and thin
Painters brush is in my hand again.
Courageous men have yet to be
Formed from the very depths of
This heart in me

Tell everyone that I,
I cannot make it home tonight

Tell everyone that I,
I cannot cry from the sky
I would not care to risk the night
From my mistakes I go and fly

People question your weakened strokes
Living off of your dying smoke again
Pour some toxic thoughts in
Your battered life just makes them choke
In their own blood

Tell everyone that I,
I cannot make it home tonight

Tell everyone that I,
I cannot cry from the sky
I would not care to risk the night
From my mistakes I go and fly

I left you all
Little notes in my blood,
Go find them in your love
Go find them in your love

I left you all
Little notes from above,
Go find them in your love
Go find them in your love

Consolation Letter for Past Iniquities

I apologize.
I truly do.
For the things I say
The actions I take.
For they are only a part of me.

My heart lives on
In the words I type
The things I scribble on
These sheets of faded paper.

And the screen I stare at
Burns the image of my mistakes
And of my dreams
Into a convoluted idea
That should not exist.

There is no chance
There is fate
There is hope
And I am late
For my mental checkup
With myself
The words are melting
Into empty bookshelves.

If I have no permanent works
If I have no physical effort
I am nothing and I am taking up air

So forgive me of past errors and ways
And I will push the barriers
Of this society
So that we can focus
And use the gifts given
And the ideas pulsating
To be released
And flourish

Oh God I need to flourish

I Cry, No Victor

I have had enough
Of this worthless poking
At my soul
With your stick fingers
With your sharp words

Oh how I want to crush you.
With every fibre I control.

OH GOD
AM I LIVING IN SIN
WHEN I SAY I WANT THIS VOICE DEAD?!
THE ONE THAT SPEAKS
IN WHISPERS AND RED

HE WANTS ME DEAD
HE WANTS ME TO FALL

OH GOD

CRUSH HIM PLEASE

I BEG YOU

I AM DOWN ON MY KNEES
BEGGING YOU

KILL THE DEVIL IN ME

BLUE:
CLARITY FALLS ON THE BLIND

Here I sit, breathing in fresh life,
Possibly for the first time.
And quiet sits my heart, waiting for revelation.

We Know, We Stare

I am not proud
Of many things that I am.
That we are.
The characteristics that we all
Close the blinds to

The damned fads
That we smile upon
But never speak of.

I humbly apologize
For the many things that I am.
Perfect is surely not one of them.
Nor is secure, or gleeful.

And lately I have been terrified
That the moment I rest my head
On the fact of my failures,
No renewal of chances will be given,
Not that I in any way deserve one.
Again.

Please note my usage of 'again'
As of late.

There is so much repetition
To life, to sin, to failure.
And few moments of clarity,
Of relief,
Of brimming hope.

I am not proud of this.
But I am aware of this.

Remove My Goggles, Sir

When I catch an idea
Drifting away
I wish to follow it
To find the destination
It craves

And usually it leads
To some horrific conclusions
That the world is empty
And I am worthless

But the scary thing is…
That I rather enjoy these moments,
As I question reality
And my place in it.

Because in those moments,
I end up realizing
That as awful as life can be
And as brutal as moments can feel
I will put my faith elsewhere
For this world holds no answers
And I can finally let go of my baggage.

…Now that I can run freely
Where should I go?

Waning, Lacking, Obsolete

The dim light carries a sound
That seldom hear
Seldom would care to hear

Who wants knowledge
In a world of instant love?

The light flickers
Casting a waning flare of insight
But waning still imbues some form of,
As this warmth still holds
And the cold still swarms
But never takes home
In my brittle bones

I scream
It flickers even more
Waning
Waning
I want the answers
But am afraid to listen
To the fading

My imperfections take form
In a lack of insight

Someday No Heroes

Eye muscles contract
Peering down with such
Arrogance
It drips and burns

All underneath
Ask for water
To ease the burns

And I hate you

They always were inclined
To your swaying walk
And comforting lies
Wearing a Lucifer grin
And a bloody hand
Full of hearts and worn hope

GIVE THEM HOPE

But every foot forward
Is one pathetic choice
As they beg you to fix
Everything

...yet you caused everything
To spiral and shake
With paranoia and such weight

Powerless they sit
Defenseless they die

They sucked up all of your lies
Drunken they die

You damn fool
Power fills words to the brim
You damned host
Serpents call you father

Quiet and Quite Rattled

My mouth
Spewing out some false bravado
I swear I love you...
But I always fall backwards
Tilting towards past whispers
And rhythmic lullabies
That were sang from above
The twisted twirling
The needed arrogance
Above the crib they shifted

...

I molded with sin
Grew through it.

So how does one rip out home
And somehow survive?

I swear my intentions were placed.

Some were in a garden of hope
Planted, redeemable.

Some were tossed to the sea
Never to return.

And the worse were not tossed.
They were placed
With open-eyed shame
In terrible moments
That I conducted
With bloodied hands,
With scarred motions.

So how does one rip out their sin
The safe net,
And somehow survive?

Elder Sounds

Harsh lighting
Purifies those pathetic thoughts
I once held with such insight

Insight on some worldview
Some panoramic shot
From great heights
Portraying the ants below
As colours in a scene

But it is all unknown

I hold love
In a mechanical place now
In a colourless mixture
Of rocks grating concrete

So I ask
(No one in particular)
If I can reach out a hand
Feel another's company
Transfix on their aura
And understand their heartaches

And maybe the colours will whisper again
Showcasing images
That I could never understand.

Could not Recall "Why"

Fingers on the keyboard,
Typing the thoughts
(As muddled as they are)
I realize my good intentions.
The crystal heart before it all.
It turns, it cracks
Under the human in me.

I am only human, they say.
I am only human, I see.
I break quite often over the small things.
I bleed frequently, it seems.

Heartfelt Echo Under Rubble

...
Crumbling down
My legs snap
Courteously leading my head
To the floor
And the 'thud'
Mars your soft ears
As the echo screams hidden pain.

I am so sorry for not crying out
Asking for something or someone.

I did not pray,
Nor ask for a helping hand.

I simply tore my own insides up
Until I coughed out crimson syrup.

Please,
Take this as a warning.
Take this as a heartfelt caution.

Ask for help
Before you die to yourself.

...one's heart can only take so much..

Black for White

Haha
I am now long gone
Forgotten,
Maybe it makes me unique
So easily replaced
So quick to whisk away

The breeze pushes past
My bones are forever
They move through the earth
Dirt & mud
I will cry underneath you all

For I am lonely
Until I awake
One day

Brighter clothes
Brighter eyes

My bones are forever

That Moment When Everything Is Clear

I am not enough.

PURPLE:
THE HEALER

Although we exist
As Skewed Entities
Wandering slanted planes of existence,
We have no need for burdens or worries.

We will be healed.
Us walking shells inherit soul.

To Ask Is To Long For

I have asked to be fixed
Because as long as this road is
And as hazy and the days are
...
I remember that we have purpose.
That my blood is in need of renewal.

I am without whole lungs,
I am without a means to breathe.
Someone push my chest, my heart
Someone carry the oxygen through me.

I have burned the worst of me
And never fully recovered.
Please...
Someone carry the oxygen through me.

These words are pathetic
Simple
Repetitive.
But I am just being honest.

I need help breathing.

Just...Can...Please...Oh My

Streamed light
Wakes the dead

Good morning.
Arise.
And leave those old homes behind
Shock fills your eyes
But no worries
You are here to stay

Pain may have broken something inside
Deep inner-workings twitch
But love
I promise,
Love will fix everything

Everything.

And as cliché as a happy heart is
...
Maybe it is not so bad to have?

Silver Needle

Flesh holds bone
In place
Understanding holds hope
In heart
Smiles hold sanity
Inside my poor head
and love holds hands
With death and art.

Life holds secrets
Behind worn eyes
That have seen too much.

Tell me,
What have you seen?

I will grab the silver needle
Stitch the open screams
And mend moments together
That purify some dreams.

Tell me what is wrong
And I will make you believe...

That you are as beautiful
As you will ever need to be.

Something, Something, Forgive Me

How many moments of clarity will it take
Before we actually act, change?

For me,
It seems eternal.

The struggle of being tired,
Worried,
Tears have left ridges
Erosion of this pale skin

I have been something else
And the words dripping out
Are not my own.

I hear awful things.
Everything my God is not.

...

And vomit creeps under each notion
As I realize I have changed.

Maybe instead of laughing it off
I should purge this heart
And start fresh

With Yahweh in mind
In heart
In soul.

I need His eyes, not my own.
Yeshua, let my words mean something.

And the Spirit can fill
The crevices left by aged tears.

Oh,
I need everything that I am not.

Something, Something, Forgive Me
(cont.)

A humble tongue.
A fruitful mind.
An ambitious heart
And a joyous spirit.

Please.

Oh, Father
Fix me.

And They Shouted, "Death Serves Us" Pt. II

But enough with this pathetic fear.
I promise to cut out my sorrows,
Vicious pests
Watch them ooze imperfections
That ran my mind red.
I will strike down emotions
Bearers of hearty devotion
To some fake things I followed.

And I will set my heart
On an uncreated Creator.

Because everything is a mess.
Everything feels so fake.

God, this stone heart needs something real.

Tumbling, Falling, Up in the Clouds

We ask.
As if asking provides a means to their torture.

Hoping for an answer.
Or heart behind the madness.

But the sun bleeds black
From the sins of our fathers
And the tears of our mothers
As they weep into the clouds.

We are alone.
Sometimes.
Do not cry, save your breath for greater.

Our breath was meant to be
Taken away by the moments
That encapsulate eternal happiness.

So breathe in,
Lose burdens,
Bleed out lost thoughts
That would otherwise
Cripple your legs
From forward motion.

Individuals.
We were not meant to be people,
But persons.

Not a group of no names,
But a collective force
Of creative minds
And outstretched hearts
Led by the numerous goals
That flare out passions
And love.

Welcome to your new self.

The Judge

Wrinkles.
My skin has folds
Ages never hold
I cannot fathom how much longer
We have to go.

I am brittle and young
So awfully high-strung
Veins changed to black
Carrying nothing these days

So please breathe life here
In this house
This town
Maybe some greener sights
Some lovely lights
A hope for tomorrow
And maybe eternity

Colour my eyes with love
Paint with strokes of red
And flesh out
A dream for this weakened humanity

Someone Had To.

So I guess it comes down to me-
To say that I am so sorry
For what the world has done to you,
How it has treated you.

I may have not lashed out like them.
...but I did not stop them either.

So please...
Just know someone cares for you.
I do, I really do.

And even if you hate me,
I will still love you
For moving forward,
For fighting onward.

I will always care.

Again, With More Feeling

The shadow of prosperity
Looms
Lingers
Can almost reach for the taste
Like mist
The particles hover
And I follow suit

Wide grin
Depth of sin
Bloody heights
All for one taste
To know life is worth it
...
Is it?

Pondering aside,
Move for the sake of motion
Until footsteps
Echo the heart's longing
Until motions
Turn to the soul's echo

I hear it now:
"You will be whole again"

PINK:
MY HEART SPEAKS OF PASSIONS

My heart ticks a beat
For the first time in years
It seems.

Unfamiliar and uncomfortable
Yet undeniably favorable.

Lingering Comfort

I cannot figure it out...

What actions did I do
To deserve being treated that way?

I know that no one deserves anything
Nothing particular
But nothing is better than
The pain she caused me
Everyday
Towards the end
Everyday
Gutting me until the end.

But it was not always that way
And my heart was not always this torn
Stab marks evident
Here is my evidence
Just look around my aura
I left what I could
To keep the poison out
I dug up my roots
But they lie deeper than words
Thicker than blood

I am scared...

I am petrified
That I will die out
Before I can become my own

Perfect Amidst Chaos

A life worth it.

To look in someone's eyes
And hear the voices no more.

That would be a life worth it.
Without the gold.
Or the fame.
Or any semblance of sanity.

But for a girl.
To have throbbing clarity
In all of the sadness
And madness
Even if it was of no benefit
To the rest of the world.

She would be worth it.

And in this moment,
I think I found hope again.

I think I will dream of her again.

Christmas Wishes, Cliché Acknowledged

I crave something.

There is this hole in my chest
Where the blood never goes
And I frequent a peak
Begging new life to take hold.

I whisper for this hole
To turn into a heart

But today is like every other
And I am just another male.

Judged like most
Dismissed like most

I beg to be seen

…and I used to question 'why'.
Why do I wish to be seen?

Then I realized that I am not
Craving a crowd of attention.

I crave love and adventure
But not with a crowd
Not with a group.

Just one.

I crave to share my life with you.

Take Me With You

Courageous enough
To present the world
With a heart of gold...

You could have left it alone
In a shell to store
All of those desires
That left you wanting more.

More...
You took that and ran towards hope.
So go and be more.
Be something the world needs,
Something the world yearns for.

Are you not that special someone?
I remember you as if a snowflake on my tongue,
A sweet reminder of where I have been
Of who I have become.

Fingers crossed that we meet again,
Serving up a better purpose,
A better zen.

And honestly...
I am astonished,
By how beautiful your chances are...
How beautiful your aura of possibilities is.

Take me with you?

Dazzled, Fallen

Did I dazzle you
With my smile?

It is all fallen nature, hun.

It is all broken dreams.
The collective pieces form something
That you call beautiful.

But this shell will not hold

And like a predator in a slaughter house
I am under the knife
Still gnashing my teeth
Breaking nothing but bones
Inside myself.

Pointless to resist.
They scream at me
To stop fighting back.

Should I give up?
Never.

You Should Know

You are beautiful.

And every time you notice it,
I see a smile,
A glimmer in your eyes.

Please never stop shining,
For there is so much out there for you.

It does not matter if I know you.

What matters is...
If you let go,
I will never get to know you.

And just the thought makes me shudder.

Please, do not forget.

You are wonderful,
And you are one of a kind.

I Wonder

Each one of us,
Filled to the brim.

Stories in heart
Scars on our skin.

These withered words
They mar young tongues.
They search for answers
Mindless and undone

Our molecular structure
Is marvelous
Yet how many days do we sob
Over the bitterness
That the world instills?

So quake at the painter's brush
Worlds created
Now you see;
Colour is never enough.

And tremble at a tender voice
Behind glassy eyes
The universe expands
She is far away, dear,
Quietly fighting demons.

Inner voices clash
Outer choices fail to match
With the heart of it all
And the somber tones
Of the parents with the dead son
Who left a lonely note
Telling them their love was not enough.

When will love be enough?
It should.

I Wonder (cont.)

Not lust,
Greed,
Or worldly joys.

But instead... love.
Love should be enough.

Too Much Yelling

He peered over the cliff
Squinting as the sun loomed overhead
Thoughts collided and he sighed.
All of his pain could end
With just one step.

Then someone walked up to him.
Past him.
She smiled at him and said "Here's to you."

She jumped so that he could see
How quickly life can end
And how soon he would regret
Even holding the thought

What Understanding Means

Shared my memories, with you on the beach
Of who we were, of who we wanted to believe in
To become them, one day
Walk further away - from our own path

One day we'll walk along the coast
Like a pair of wolves, yeah we're guarded most
By our memories, that have yet to be
Parched lips cry out for flooded dreams

Life flood on me

Reality was never a thing
Remember the weak that brought a sting
On our brass minds
Yeah we wanted most what was left behind
In the fading ages

One day we'll walk along the coast
Like the quiet hum, I'm hated most
By their judging ears, by their judging minds,
Parched lips cry out for flooded dreams

Life flood on me, life flood on me, life flood on me...

Shared my memories, with you in the grass
The cars they moved along, but their lights held fast
To our brown eyes, all night
Held closer to sight - than our own path

Go walk the fence, I'll stay behind
Never meant to be, your hand in mine
But I sit and stare, so go places unknown
Yeah I wonder where

Remember the time we walked the coast?
Like a trusted soul, I'm used the most
By your crying eyes, don't look behind
Parched lips cry out for flooded dreams

Don't forget that whats guarded most
Tried to bury my love, in your button coat
But you left me dry

Go walk the world, I'll stay behind
Never again to see, Your brown eyes
Go walk the line, of whats white and black
Don't turn back, hun, don't turn back.

Life flood on me

You Lied. I Sighed.

A walk in the park
Bodies on the verge of friction
As we smiled so close to each other...
The trees silenced themselves in anticipation
...for the next moment.
But it never came.
I was so startled by the chemicals mixing,
By our chemical reaction,

...

That I did not notice you leave for the crowd
Hoping to lose me amidst the commotion.
But why such a commotion?
Everyone is amuck
Yet this scene is barren of sound

And then it occurred to me;
they are all carrying knives,
Looking at me with malevolent intent

God, where do I go?
These strangers want blood
And my passions scurried amongst them

Like dye running through hair
The stains of her existence are apparent:
Both in me and this swarm, tumbling towards me.

...And each wound these souls open in me,
Each colour of feeling that I see,
Is another reminder of how passionate love can be,

And how you perplex the greatest of us all.

An Idea To Send Off

Forgive this fog,
Please. It knows no better.

I would travel the world,
Near and far,
Just to find your heart.

And in that deepest crevice,
Where all hate gathers,
I will pluck up your innocence,
Dust off the ingenuity
and the wit,
And show you where they belong.

With me.

Your darkest features
They deserve a home, too.
I will be there for the malice
and the hate.
I will smile through the lingering poison
Born from your harshest desires.

And I will continue to hold through it all.
Because I know how much you are worth,
Better than any other soul.
So let me show you.

I will speak of your worth,
Until you wear robes laden with it,
Believing it to be truth.
It honestly is.

And you are worth it.

GREY:
SMUDGES

This twitching mind
Overflows with imperfections.

Yet I assure you this one simple concept:
Fears and disasters are mere stepping stones
When passions guide me onward.

So Long, My Fears

If I dared to go
Where my eyes roam

Blue seas
The beyond

Maybe I would shed this rotten skin
And find a home in the unknown
Delving further from comfort
Delving further to peel away
Some worthless clichés
And lingering hate.

If I dared to fly
Where my soul drifts

Blue skies
The beyond

Maybe I would comprehend
How perfect we are made
And how little we need to change
To be something short of a miracle

You are so beautiful
Just smile more
I am still lacking
But I think I will pray more.

And I will grow wings.

For the Dears and the Disasters

Her arm out the window
Switchblade in hand
She cuts the air
It bleeds a thought
And begs for more
Wanting attention
From this beautiful girl

Her arm stretches out
Switchblade in hand
Further she aims
For the sun and the sky
The moon behind
The outlying stars
She knows it belongs to her.

Passion is carried through her veins
Wisdom trickles from each thought
Produced,
How gorgeous wisdom is.

Her arm wraps the universe
Switchblade in hand

What is to stop this?

Nothing should.
Maybe we need a wakeup call

Hurricane, Cleanse It

I think that my mind has been refreshed.

The wants and needs
Of this unkempt life
All swarm in my skull
Writhing
Yearning to find a new home.

And maybe I will calm down,
Replay any moments of sanity
Relapse back into a madman
And then curse myself for the thought.

Black and white are words
Not actions.
Grey defines the moral choices
With the colours of the rainbow
Holding tight as emotional voices.

Red for the bitter rage
Blue for the harsh reality
Green for the lusts and haze
Orange for the passion
Yellow for the puking submission
Purple for my royal mistakes

And most importantly
Pink for some love I once had
And thoughts I kept dear.

Grey defines the moral choices

Precisely Answered

I am revolted
By this spinning.
By my careless laughing
Of this evening.

Cords tangling
My brain with my heart
These Living signals
Awry
Bleaching my eyes
Of all knowledge
I once held dear.

If we are to hold wisdom dear
To our chest,
Does this make our hearts wise?

If we are to sing songs of hope
Are we then hopeful?

Going through the motions
I pray motions turn to meaning.

...because without meaning
One could look up and see
The birds in the sky
Losing hope as well
Direction of humble endings
Falling falling
All things rotting
Corrupt your mind
Without meaning
Life has no calling.

Find a calling
Hold dear
Hold dear

Find your heart
and never let it go.

Tears and Smiles

I could swear that I felt movement
Inside of my insidious bones
Inside of my wretched spine

The chill of a new idea
Crawls up my pathetic skin
And once it clicks in this skull
A smile creeps up my cracking face.

I can exist again.

Better.
Brighter.
Stronger of mind
And sure of intent.

Something is coming
And I am ready.

I will start to break myself free
Of this mold
Of this mainframe

And beg to be reborn.

But I do not just beg.
I act.
I will act.

I will be a phoenix
And this is my rebirth.

This is, You are, We will

Maybe one more
Moment set aside
To quiet my heart
(And all of my insides)

Oh how life grips tender strings
To shock these hands
Into submission and guilt.
And guilt. And guilt.

Write write write
Sketch and etch they say
These thoughts are corroding in my skull
Seeping out to my soul

So sweep me up,
Calm this bitter moment
And I can be more than I ever imagined.

Smile bright
Calm my heart,
Please.

You are irresistible
And I am swarming with infinite colours.

Some Vicious Circle

It has been so long
And the journey so cold
Yes,
My fingers fall off
And my heart wears old

Heavy are my thoughts
Heavy feelings of regret
Maybe life is better somewhere else
Maybe life could leave me
Blooming instead of perpetually fading

But these roots dug deep
From the years of compliance
The soil holds firm
To all of my toils and reliance
On everyone else
-to tell me who I am
Yes everyone else
Please let go
I do not wish for helping hands

I am not bulletproof
But maybe I can try
To shake off these bullet holes
Pretend they are not mine

The blood is not gone
It just resides elsewhere
The holes can be padded
Just as my mind can be mended.

Okay,
I suppose my words fell sour
On even my tongue...
I really do need a helping hand,
But then I will move on.

Nothings

Why do I not see a muse
Anymore?
Can I not search my heart
And produce honest words?

I am withered
Yes,
I am weakened
Heart is irregularly torn
Yet I am still breathing

Maybe even breathing itself
Is a sign for higher reason
To push forward
To move onward?

And accented by cold surroundings
I find myself drowning
In hope
Despite sometimes feeling alone.

Knowledge of my humanity,
It grants me grace
Once again.

I am not perfect
Nor will I ever be.

So I will try to be
Proficient, kind, loving,
And understanding.

Let me not write for them
Or even monetary gain…
But for some form of love
Some form of hopeful standing.

Let me write
For hope that I can flourish.

A Single Lit Match

I realize how broken we all are.

So why...
...why do we belittle each other?
Beat each other up even more?
The world sobs in a state of conviction
-we know what we have done
So know now that there is time to change.

Why the need for dominance and fighting?
How many loved ones have risked their blood
For a country's selfish gain?

Maybe we cannot rebuild our government.
But we as humans can rearrange our hearts...
To look like hearts.

And our faces to have genuine smiles.

Imagine that.
Seeing someone genuinely smile at you.
Why not try it?

Not tomorrow. Now.
Today. Whenever you see someone next.

Hug your family or friends.

Be genuine.
Please.

Sense(s)

A quick headcount of these
Mumbling voices
One two three
Stop.
These are not my choices
Not yet

Trickling lies
Peer from the corners
Of a room in my head

The shadows persist
Mind numbing games,
They insist
That maybe the media is right
Or
Maybe my voice is not really mine
as I look back with poor hindsight.

I do not wish to be a puppet.
I do not wish to be spoon fed.

Plural
I am the problem
Singular
We are the solution
Inquiring a summary
Of this jumbled up psychosis
For moments that
We are not even in synch with.

Nothing can clear our minds
Better than stepping outside

Nothing can stop their voices
Better than finding your own

More than Here

A moment to think
And I am off and away.

A moment to think
And I am off and away.

WHITE:
REBIRTH

Stop chasing ghosts,
Fleeting memories
Of mistakes.

The earth begs for change.

Let Me Live

I find a deep urge
To explore
To be
To breathe
And find purpose.

But don't we all?

So what makes me any different?

At this young age
We feel immortal
We talk with viper's words
And bleeding eyes
Seeing through our pain and love
As key benefactors
For all perfection and hate

And even though I look up to the sky
What is the point?

I am the cause of these scars
And bloodied hands
I am the reason I hurt
And continue to hurt

So I will clean these cuts
With my own acidic words
Burn old photos
I longingly held close
. . .
And then I will run towards hope
Gain momentum
Break out of this cell
Colliding with broken glass
Of the old windowpane

Let me be honest...
You never know what awaits you
Until you jump through

Let Me Live (cont.)

And the air fills my lungs
More potent
More pure
...
I think that I am living now

It Ends in Awe

All experiences provide tints
Every muse colours the same scene
With different eyes

We were meant to love

Whether it is found in desperation,
Lonely cries
Whit and charm,
Or an adventurous lust
For something different.

We were formed
And we will decompose.
But the words you say
Imprint the soft earth
From sand to dirt.

So find love...
In art and literature,
Sobering tones of the rain,
A humble view of the sky or sea
And lift up your eyes to the heavens

Everything was made so beautiful
And we were molded to admire it

Myself Included

Be cautious
Be controlled
Never let words leave your mind
Until your heart defines their purpose.

Do not scratch and tear
With uncontrolled thoughts
As even a guarded heart
Is weaker than it cares to admit.

Instead,
Rebuke pathetic notions
Leave room for improvement,
Harden your heart to bickering
And love all
Regardless of any reciprocation.

Maybe then we can understand what love is.

Wires and Dancing

And this is our moment.

With so many changes
With so many catalysts

Who are we to stay stone?

Not only do I beg for change
But the earth does, too.

It cries out to be heard
To be understood.

And it reflects its Maker's intent.

Beauty is overwhelming
And I am on my knees

How can existence be so beautiful
Even amidst chaos and blood?

How can the world hum on
As we kill each other
In greed and agony?

Who are we to stay stone?
I promise to cut myself free
And replace this stone core

Feeling Lesser

The world revolts
Not knowing a true name,
Lashing out with fire and poison
...
When did we forget about love?
Why did we forget about compassion?

The lust for money
Rots skin.

Hands shaking
Laughing, Ticking-
The sounds of head trauma
From many failed dreams.

If only our hearts resided
Where our words pretend to go.

Places of hope.

But instead we bleed animosity
Picking open wounds
Seething with venomous whispers.

Is it so wrong
To want a brighter tomorrow?

Listening To Your Old Recordings

Bleached mind and clear skies
The world awaits
The heart of a passionate man
The soul of a borderless smile...

So why have you not moved?
Why do words lead to nothing more
Than a few nods and waves.
At best.
But this is far worse.

Feet scuff the floors
Of your worn out living room
Irony
You have yet to live

Would it not be better
To die in passion
Than never live,
Trapped in an outward representation
Of your dusty soul?

Currents pull me onward
The grin of my heart pours outward
Oh God I think I am finally free

Why do they all look?
No wave,
Not hoping
Simply staring at my heart
Ten sizes of what it used to be.

After the currents lead me to passion
They all await another
Just like before
Maybe one more
And they will follow
But one more is for the future
And the future is but a worthless idea.

And you are far from worthless.
You are not an idea.

You are two hearts set in motion
Producing hope and inspiring more
More and more
Become that more
And maybe you can follow me to passion
Maybe we all can.

Please.
No need to hide in a crowd.
Let them watch,
Amazed

Let them live again
For the first time
Because the first
Was broken

Become that more
That you were born to be

Follow onward
Passion
Pain
Sorrow.

It is all better than nothingness.
It shines brighter than any false light.

And you are far from false light.
You are bright

Screaming Souls

As the days pass
I document the changing aura
Of this battered soul.

Many emotions swirl,
Churning my stomach until I fade
Leaving few moments of sanity
Leaving many nights of bewildered haze

So instead of moving on without purpose
I decide to find myself...
To realize I am not worthless

Collect the heartfelt thoughts
Stomach the hurt
Stomach the loss

We are so worried about tomorrow
About the past
About ailments

Should we not smile for the fact
That we are alive? Living? Breathing?

Nothing is chance,
Everything has beauty
You are worth it
Just find your inner beauty

Leave the Ocean, Find a Home

No
I will not stay
I will not mourn

I will uproot this life
I will stand for something

And more importantly,

I will be someone,
Not this hollow shell
Drowning in my filth.

I will be unique,
And I will be only known as 'me'.

Burn my masks
Leave it as offering
Let the aroma cleanse
Let the charred remains sing

I will not follow some idols
I will not move for lust or greed.

I will be unique
Created by the Uncreated Creator

And I will be only known as 'me'

Poor Kings and Purification

I am leaving the scenery.

The tragic skyscraper
I once loved to climb
Footprints melted in
The sun held some thin-
-layer of sanity
Some thin layer of reality
(But not enough to look down)

I should ponder if this
If this is any better
The new surroundings
I bursted into
With harsh steps
That were deliberate
Yet unguided...

Okay.
Catching my breath,
No worries mar my chest
No weight to smooth over
Cling over
Or breathe harsher from.

I take in forestry
The scandalous idea of running again...
It pleases me
Although even this was better than "it",
Being the pit I dug myself years ago.

Come to think of it,
That pit was better suited as a grave.
But not for me.
Someone else can take on that role.

With the world in front of me
I realize this is not a picture.
It is reality,
And I can react with and to reality.

It begs me to affect it, distort it,
...
Forever change it.

And I will.

But not like another.

I will be the rock
That starts a ripple.

And so I throw myself towards
The heart of it all.

Towards Infinite

Can I be honest with you?
Whoever peers onto these pages
And drinks in my madness…

I wanted to say something.

Whether or not your life has been a mess,
It does not matter.

What matters is where you go from here.

So step outside,
Look at your feet,
Pull out your roots
And follow your heart.
Your passions.
Any dreams.

A world filled with passion
Is much richer
Than a world filled with perfection.

So move.

And watch the grace follow.

PREVIEW:

WRECK, REBIRTH
A DARK COLLECTION OF SHORT STORIES AND POETRY
TO BE RELEASED WINTER 2015

Was this place actually haunted? The teenage students mumbled between each other while hiking up the outer hills. Ruins of a rustic adjoined town laid ahead, where absolutely no one was allowed to venture in. The twenty-or-so young classmates calmed their steps as they reached "limbo" - what almost everyone called the seventy miles separating home from the nearest functional towns. Crouching, several of them perched their ears towards the sky. They listened intently, eyes darting sporadically while waiting for any sign of unwanted guests – especially of the authoritative type. The rhythmic sound of nature slowly filled in as their other senses faded for the time being. A few students sighed in relief. Others sighed in failed hopes of being caught and sent back with a slapped wrist by a set or two of stern eyes. The homely lights of their fading town fell mute on the back of their necks as if an indication of separation anxiety. This trek marked the furthest that most of them had ever dared to wander. In unison they pushed onward, albeit in a timely manner. Dusk approached in tender pace, seeping both shadow and light in equal affair. The moon shined out in quiet desperation as nature fell to darkened desires. The night moved on, as did the peering faces and trembling hands. Although it was relatively quiet in limbo, the ruins ahead echoed something sinister. Something had rustled beyond the nearing tree line that divided them from the ruins. The majority of students did not even acknowledge the sound. That, or the more likely alternative: it was only heard by a few individuals because the world is an uncomfortable place holding uncomfortable motives. It had provoked a few teens from the larger group to meet together. Whispering amongst each other, they questioned if the noise was widely heard or not. Only three friends in the group had actually heard the noise. The others, except for one, laughed it off as a failed joke. Some obscene gestures were thrown as they circled back into the larger cluster. One teen held back with the three friends. He wanted to know what existed beyond the pines. After a few nods they had decided to move. Onward they ventured past the tree line. Past safety. Past existence.

One student in particular wore a rather unnerving expression. Henry. His smile sat coldly and his gait was ethereal. Had the darkened skies and accompanying shadows not slipped over his face, someone might have questioned his purpose there. Surely it was not to wander, to explore, to discover. No, it was to track down the voices that called out to him in growing agony. And if any one had known that Henry frequented this site weekly, it might have caused a stir and shift in attention. He stood amongst the others purely to observe the results of this damned night. His dark-brown hair fluttered mutely as his blue eyes keened on surrounding shadows. He did not join the prying bunch as they delved into unknown land. Instead, he hovered near the main cluster of glittery eyes and stuttering mouths. Soon the prying bunch would find home in the belly of the monsters that hunkered nearby – that hungered nearby – that breathed in with anticipation nearby.

Oh my.

Henry did not exist.

…at least not in a traditional sense. There were days when he would regressed into a state of being 'real' – moments where he could almost forget the puking and bitter words that frothed over the old man's pale lips. Bastard. Tick tock. But those days grew further and further apart, like lighting dashing through the heavens, far-removed from the metal rod that it should call comfort. That it should call home. Pain took form in a stark realization that normally would not have hit for many, many years. Between the repressed images and seeping lies, Henry had forgotten what the truth was anymore. But did it matter? The disconnect from everything else was a layer he wore with comfort now. He found his answers in whispers and unnatural habits. Tick.

Clumsily, the four classmates kept trekking onward. Through several elder pines they wandered, fighting away branches and flies. The distraction of pine needles scraping skin had probably kept them from focusing on what each footstep represented; each ill-placed step was a louder drum beat, quickly pacing towards an abrupt moment. A brutal stop. The remaining classmates watched from a distance, shooting concerned-yet-savage glances towards each other. No one said that they wanted this to end in blood. But blood was surely more brilliant than the lackluster ending that everyone sadly awaited. The four teens went out of focus and eventually sight. On cue Henry split off on his own, passing the tree line a few yards to their left. Finding comfort between two small ferns near the burial site, he rested on the ground in humble anticipation. The anxious teens peered into view and began to wander about, unaware of Henry's intent or existence. Tock tick.

And then it began. No room for questions or even the spark of thought. The four teens were swiftly snatched up and not-so-swiftly consumed. Henry watched from between the ferns. A single "Holy-" left one of the boys' mouths as it was torn from his face, along with his entire lower jaw. There was nothing holy about this place. Everything else happened in an almost delicate silence. *Why not observe the rare events that grace this world?* Tonight was the first time that his ritual had worked. This. **THIS.** *THIS* was something that few ever had the chance to witness. The main group of students were still paused moments behind, living a healthier existence, a healthier frame of mind. They began to separate into their cliques, bickering amongst themselves over "who could climb the highest", and "who could stand in the darkness the longest." Beyond the withered pines a few arm-spans from them sat the ruins of many abandoned buildings. Graffiti littered the scenery. But some words had purpose beyond rebellion. Some colours melded too well within the crumbling walls. Some reds were too perfect... and some places are better left untouched. These children lacked common knowledge of the land that they had crossed into. The burial ground. Tock.

It seemed as if the shadowy beasts were satisfied. And there was Henry. Quiet. Observant. Distant in nature and heaving in ecstasy. These creatures were pleasure-seekers too, he could tell. Snarling in satisfaction but never having enough. The three beasts spoke amongst themselves in foreign tongue as mixed blood and mashed bones sloshed around their inhuman cavernous mouths. Twitching, their bloodlust picked up another human. Except... there was no pounce. There were no teeth to young flesh. The beasts looked right into his damned soul. A shaking tension caused Henry to giggle. He had no clue what to do. No gifts, no show of peace. No show of *respect. But then it clicked.* So he bowed and then proceeded to softly spin in circles, melding the stars into lines and shapes far above. It truly was some kind of love. He was not meandering for words to say as flesh separated and dissolved. He simply smirked. He was inspired. It was *just* what he needed. Tick tick tick.

He simply smirked.

Tick tick ring

.tock.

ring ring ring

He awoke, bed dampened by tears. But Henry was not sobbing. His alarm kept trilling with its rhythmic chaos… and he was laughing to himself, almost in sync with the alarm. The dream was inspiration. Wishful thinking, actually. Weeks had gone by without a reply. This was as close as he would ever get. Mechanically, he emerged from bed and began to clothe. This was a special night. It marked the anniversary of the incident. The taste of blood still lingered, marring every day with a crimson tinge and array of thoughts. Henry licked his lips. After donning the proper attire and placing a rushed note on the couch, he walked outside and closed the wooden door. Frigid air rushed past his soulless hands. Indeed, this was a very special night.

…would you like to know where this began?

TO BE RELEASED WINTER 2015

Made in the USA
Middletown, DE
14 August 2015